4 029943 002 C0

WAGON WHEELS
Roll West

Written by Neil and Ting Morris
Illustrated by Anna Clarke
Historical advisor: Marion Wood

Evans Brothers Limited

Published by Evans Brothers Limited
2A Portman Mansions, Chiltern Street
London W1M 1LE

© Neil Morris and Anna Clarke 1988

All Rights Reserved. No part of this publication may be reproduced, stored in a retrieval system, or transmitted, in any form or by any means, electronic, mechanical, photocopying, recording or otherwise, without prior permission of Evans Brothers Limited.

First published 1988

Printed in Hong Kong by Wing King Tong Co. Ltd.

ISBN 0 237 50972 5

INTRODUCTION

A new nation was born in 1783 when the Revolutionary War ended and the United States gained independence. At that time the western boundary was formed by the Mississippi River. Beyond that was a vast wilderness, the home of wild animals and nomadic tribes of Plains Indians.

In 1803 the United States made the Louisiana Purchase, buying over 2 million square kilometres of land from the French. For an agreed sum of 15 million dollars, this deal more than doubled the territory of the previous 17 states of the young republic. The new land stretched westwards from the Mississippi to the Rocky Mountains. Soon daring pioneers and fur trappers started forging trails into the forests, mountains and deserts of this unmapped new territory.

From 1840 thousands of families travelled along the Oregon and California trails to the far West to seek a new life. The early pioneers travelled towards a land that was largely unknown, with no maps or journals to guide them. Families of pioneers joined together for safety, but the wagon trains faced a difficult, dangerous journey. Not everyone made it to their intended new home.

This is the story of one pioneer family, and their adventures on the long journey west. The information pages with the rifle border will tell you more about the life and work of the pioneers of the American West.

The long line of wagons moved slowly through the wilderness.
When they reached the river, the oxen plunged in
and the wagon wheels rumbled over the stony bottom.
Anna was walking next to her father, when the wagon jolted
to a halt. He pushed hard, but the wagon would not shift.

'Another broken axle,' Anna's father said. 'Take Beth and the boys and follow the others,' said her mother. 'We'll soon catch up with you.' 'I want my spade,' Bob cried. He never went anywhere without it, just in case he came across gold.

'Don't cry, Beth,' Anna said gently, 'we are going to the promised land.' This is what their father had told them when they set off on the trail to Oregon. There they would have their own farm, but it was such a long journey.

The wagon

- feed trough
- toolbox
- brake lever
- tar pot
- water keg

The wagon was a home on wheels, a hospital and a fortress. Oxen pulled the wagons which carried the family's furniture, food supplies, cooking equipment and other essential belongings.

Families of pioneers joined together for safety and went in groups of at least ten wagons. The wagon train set off in spring from outfitting towns like Independence and St. Joseph in Missouri. The journey took about five months. The travellers elected a wagon master, and mountain men acted as scouts and guides. The first families travelled to Oregon in 1839, and to California a year later.

With the new axle there were no more breakdowns. It was Jim's turn to steer the wagon, as father looked through the spyglass. 'Can you see the others?' Jim shouted. He too had seen a huge cloud of dust.

There was no time to explain. A herd of buffalo was charging straight towards them. Father cracked his whip and Jim drove the wagon hard. They had to get out of the way fast!

When they had caught up with the others, Anna saw how lucky they had been. Some had lost all their belongings. Anna felt proud of her father. They would always be safe with him. The boys were enjoying the freshly cooked buffalo meat, but Anna kept thinking of the huge brown animals thundering past.

On the move

The pioneers took clothes, blankets, tents and spare parts for the wagon. They made sure they had enough food to last five to six months. On the plains they killed buffalo for fresh meat. They also took cattle to provide meat and milk.
1 wagon; 2 spyglass; 3 lantern; 4 medicine box; 5 sewing box; 6 butterchurn; 7 axe; 8 cradle; 9 bucket; 10 washtub; 11 quilt and mattress; 12 reflector oven; 13 iron; 14 skillet; 15 whetstone and knife; 16 pewter plates; 17 spade; 18 patent leather cups; 19 camp stool; 20 chamber pot; 21 trunk; 22 coffee pot.

They pressed on to reach the fort before nightfall. 'You'll never get those wagons over the mountains,' the trappers warned them. 'Indian tribes are on the war path, defending their hunting grounds.' Anna watched the Indian girl and her child. Why couldn't they be friends, she wondered.

It had not rained for days, and as they climbed they got further and further away from the river. The children were thirsty, but they said nothing. They knew that the last waterskin must be kept for baby Beth.

That night Anna heard her father tell her mother that he could not go on guard duty. His face was as white as chalk. 'You'll feel better in the morning,' mother said. 'I'll look after things.'

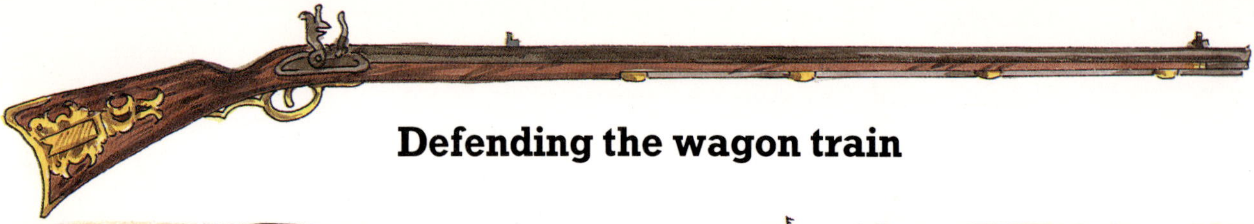

Defending the wagon train

Wagon trains needed to be constantly on the watch for bands of hostile Indians. Lone wagons were an easy target for Indian war parties. At night the wagons were formed into a circle, which served as a corral for the animals and a fortress against attack.

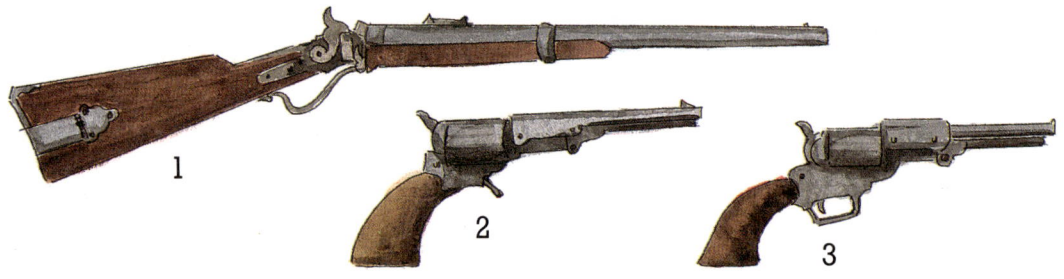

If Indians attacked, the pioneers defended themselves from behind the barrier of wagons. Although at first the Indians were armed only with bows and arrows, lances and tomahawks, they could shoot eight arrows in the time it took to load the pioneers' rifles.
1 Sharps carbine; 2 Paterson Colt; 3 Walker Colt.

But next morning father was worse, and they could not move on. 'I'll find gold,' Bob said, 'then we can buy medicines for father.' Anna did not have the heart to remind her little brother that there were no stores in the wilderness.

Jim brought some cactus leaves. 'They taste sweet and juicy,' he said. The children were all chewing when their mother came out of the wagon. She did not have to say anything – they knew at once. Father was dead.

They had to catch up with the other wagons. Mother placed a cross where they buried father. 'Now he'll never see the promised land,' Anna thought, and felt drops on her cheeks. 'Rain!' Jim shouted. They had not said a word since father died. Bob licked the rain. 'We'll be all right,' mother said.

A terrible storm raged all night. Outside, their frightened animals panted in terror. Suddenly they heard the howl of a wolf. It came from beneath the wagon. There was a rustling sound. 'It's coming in!' Bob screamed.

'Don't shoot!' Jim cried, 'it's a boy!' The Indian child looked terrified, but he was glad for the shelter the family offered. When the storm stopped, he took off his moccasins and gave them to Jim. Then he left as suddenly as he had appeared.

The fort

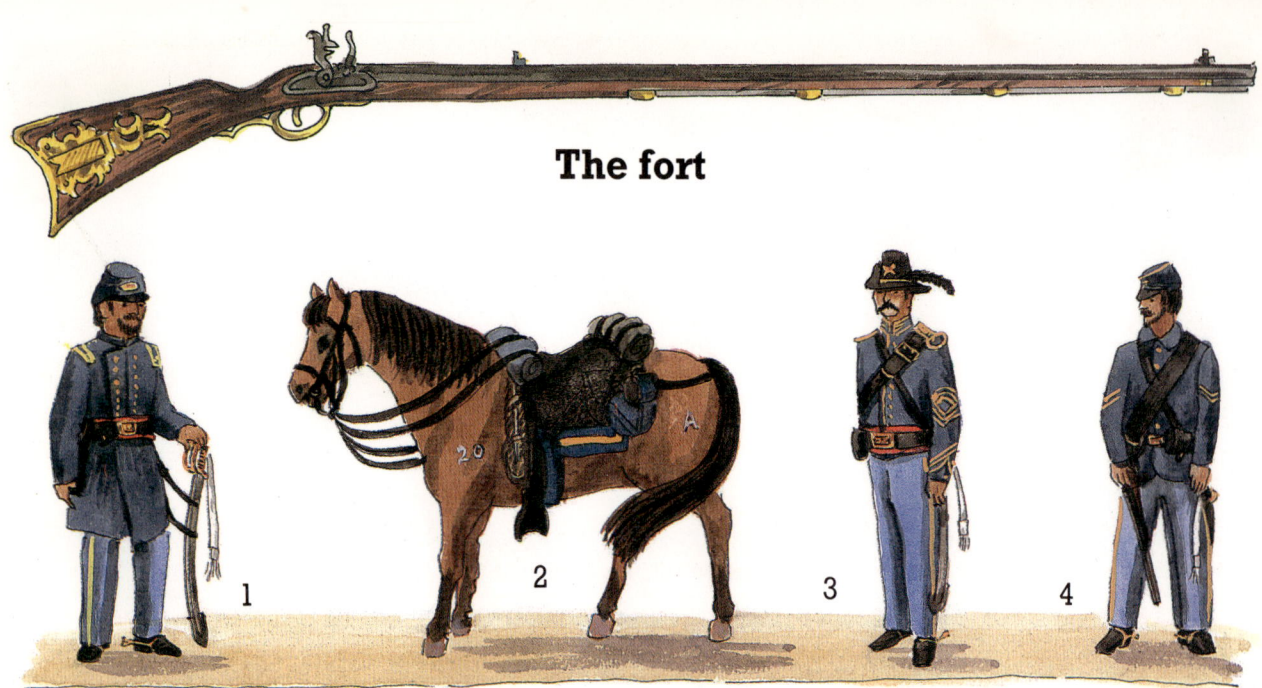

The United States Cavalry (soldiers on horseback) helped to keep law and order in the Old West, and fought in the wars against the Indians. They were armed with sabres, revolvers and carbines.
1 Major, Third Cavalry; 2 calvalry horse; 3 Sergeant Major, Second Dragoons; 4 Corporal, Second Dragoons.

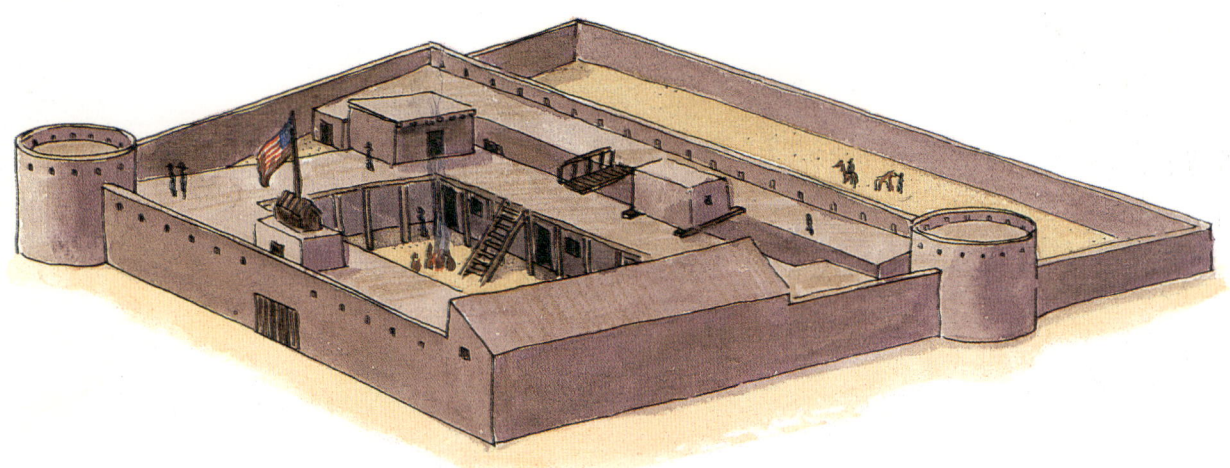

The Cavalry were stationed in forts such as Fort Laramie. As well as being military posts, the forts were used as trading places. They were also resting points and supply stations for pioneer wagon trains heading west.

The journey was much easier now. Jim wore his Indian moccasins all the time. When they saw smoke rising behind the hill, Bob said: 'Why can't we go to that Indian village? I want moccasins too, my shoes are all torn.' Mother promised to make moccasins for all of them.

She did not tell the children that she could no longer make out any trail, and there was no trace of the other wagons. All she thought of was getting across the icy streams before snow blocked the passes. Already the nights were freezing.

By now they had lost their cattle and made the wagon into a cart. Whenever they climbed one mountain ridge, there was another one ahead. But this time they could not believe what they saw – gold prospectors.

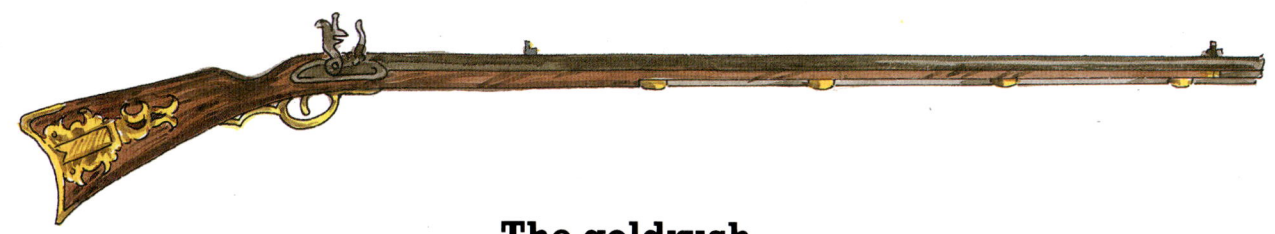

The goldrush

In 1848 gold was discovered at a sawmill in California, and when the news got out, people were gripped by 'gold fever'. The big rush started in the spring of 1849, but many of the 'Forty-Niners', as these gold-seekers became known, did not strike it rich. One man in every five died. Gold camps soon dotted the West. Prospectors panned the rivers and mined the hills for gold-rich pebbles.

Miners sifted the sand from the river-bed with metal pans. Heavy gold dust settled at the bottom.

Rockers were used to separate gold from the gravel.

In a sluice box a constant flow of water washed the gravel; the waterwheel sped up this operation.

'There is enough gold for all,' the prospectors said. But the children knew that their mother would not join the gold-diggers. They were bound for Oregon and the farm. While they mended their wagon and clothes, Bob went off with his spade to dig for gold.

'Why couldn't we stay with them?' Bob moaned. 'We wouldn't have found gold anyway,' his mother consoled him. 'I found some,' the boy said and pulled out a gold nugget.

The boys and baby Beth always fell asleep straight away, but Anna tried to stay awake. She hated the howl of the wolves, and mother never dared put the rifle down. They all missed father terribly.

They kept going day after day, through snow and ice, climbing ridge after mountain ridge. And suddenly they reached the last one. Far below them lay a green valley. 'Oregon,' mother said, 'where we will have our own farm.' Together they walked down the last slope into their new life.

This map of the American West shows the trails travelled by the pioneers across the Western plains to reach Oregon, California and Salt Lake City.